FOOD AND FARMING

John Baines

Contents

Introduction   6

Our Global Food Store   8

Globalisation and Free Trade   12

Food Producers Around the World   18

Food for the Global Market   24

Can Free Trade be Fair Trade?   30

The Future of Farming   36

The Great Debate   42

Facts and Figures   43

Further Information   44

Glossary   45

Index   46

Introduction

Today, it is possible to produce fresh food in one country and sell it anywhere in the world. It is just as likely that green beans sold in a supermarket have been grown in Africa as on a farm nearby. This is an example of globalisation. Globalisation is both an idea and an activity. Many business people and politicians believe that individuals and national economies can benefit from the free movement of goods and services between countries. This is known as trade. When the idea is put into practice, though, it can be more complicated. While some people benefit, others can end up worse off.

▲ Many people in MEDCs today buy their food from supermarkets. Globalisation has allowed produce from all over the world to be made available to consumers.

Feeding the world

Technological advances are making it easier for people to travel, communicate and do business internationally, and it is these advances that are helping a new rapid expansion of globalisation in food and farming. Everyone needs food, and adequately feeding a human population that now exceeds six billion represents a huge challenge. It also creates a big business opportunity for food and farming companies.

International trade

International trade in food products is likely to continue to grow, but the trade is small compared with the total amount of food produced. Nine out of every 10 tonnes of food produced in the world are used within the country that produces them. Furthermore, much of the food is consumed by the families that produce it. This happens most in less economically developed countries (LEDCs), where a higher proportion of the population lives in rural areas. These people are dependent upon what their patch of land can supply. In more economically developed countries (MEDCs) the situation is very different. There are few farmers. People buy their food from shops, especially supermarkets. Consumers know little about the quality of the food they buy, how it is grown, or if the producer is receiving a fair price for it. Generally they will choose what looks good and is cheapest.

This book is about the globalisation of food and farming – the trade of food and food products between countries. It will look at the rules that affect the trade of food products and the way those rules impact on the lives of people, the environment and the economies of the countries involved. All these issues raise several questions about the effects that globalisation is having in this sector, including the role played by international organisations and multinational business corporations.

Focus on...
A world of farmers

Farming is still the biggest single occupation over the globe as a whole. The 10 countries with the highest percentage of farmers are all LEDCs. Most MEDCs are urbanised, with fewer people working on the land. For example, Belgium is the most urbanised country of any size, with 97.4 per cent of the population living in towns. In North America, 67 per cent of people live in towns and in Europe 53 per cent, compared with 45 per cent in Latin America, 18 per cent in Asia and 16 per cent in Africa.

▲ Bhutan has the highest percentage of farmers in the world, and the country's economy relies on the income generated through agriculture.

Country	Percentage of farmers	No. of farmers in millions
Bhutan	93	0.94
Burkina Faso	92	5.06
Nepal	92	10.11
Burundi	90	3.02
Rwanda	90	3.73
Niger	87	4.39
Ethiopia	82	22.89
Guinea-Bissau	82	0.45
Mali	80	4.50
Uganda	80	9.13

▲ This chart shows the 10 countries with the highest percentage of farmers according to their population.

Eyewitness

Elizabeth Leitzell, an American student, is concerned that global companies such as Starbucks can reduce the amount of choice available to consumers:

'Let's look at Seattle as a case study. Once upon a time, Seattle was known for having a coffee shop on every block – you had a choice of Seattle's Best Coffee, Starbucks, Tully's, Espresso Roma, Café Ladro ... the list went on and on. Now, Seattle has over 90 Starbucks locations, not including all the grocery stores and malls with booths. Tully's is bankrupt, Seattle's Best was just bought by Starbucks and many of the independent coffee shops have gone under.'

Our Global Food Store

Humans eat a greater variety of foods than most other animals. These foods can come from many parts of the world. What we buy and how much it costs is largely controlled by government policies, international commodity markets (a commodity is any item that can be traded for another) and trade agreements.

Growing food

Humans can eat a wide variety of foods, including fruit, vegetables, meat, fish, seeds, and animal by-products such as butter, milk, cheese and eggs. What we eat is usually what we have become accustomed to. Food is an important part of different cultures, and countries have their own styles of cuisine. Some – such as French, Chinese, Indian and Italian – now enjoy international popularity. In MEDCs people are becoming more adventurous in what they eat, and this often means exotic foods are imported from countries thousands of kilometres away.

Another reason for eating foods grown in other countries is that plants grow best in certain soils and weather conditions. When it is cold, plants stop growing altogether. For example, temperate areas such as northern Europe have warm and cool seasons. Not much grows in the winter season, while there is a profusion of fruit and vegetables available in summer and autumn. However, during winter, the summer produce can be grown in places closer to the Equator, where temperatures are higher, or even in the opposite hemisphere, where it is summer.

▲ Many cities all over the world now have a 'Chinatown', like this one in Los Angeles, United States, where people can experience Chinese culture and cuisine.

Transporting food

Food products can be transported fresh in cooled containers, making it possible to buy most foods at any time of the year. Expensive, perishable foods such as fresh strawberries are often carried by air to reach the market quickly, while lower-priced vegetables with a longer shelf life, such as potatoes, are more likely to be transported by train or lorry. Have you ever thought how far your food has travelled before you eat it? While it is obvious that apples from New Zealand have travelled half way around the world to be eaten in Europe, it may not be so obvious that food produced locally could also have had a very long journey. It may have been collected from the farm, transported to a central depot of the supermarket for weighing and wrapping, and then taken back to a supermarket close to where it was grown. The distance the food travels in its journey from the farm to the supermarket shelves is known as 'food miles'.

The main argument for eating local food and reducing food miles is that it cuts down on transport. This uses less fossil fuels, which are a major cause of global warming. Eating local food also supports local farmers and the communities in which they live.

Focus on...
Food miles

Transport is only one area in which food production and consumption affects the environment. New Zealand exports fruit, dairy products and meat to other continents, and so the food miles count is very high. However, New Zealand farmers generally apply few fertilisers. Also, livestock such as dairy cattle are able to graze outside all year round. In Europe and North America animals often have to be fed on concentrated feed, especially during the winter. Much of this is imported from South America and Asia. When all the energy used by the time the food is eaten is added up, produce from New Zealand can actually be more energy efficient than buying local produce in Europe.

Have your say

The cost of fuel used to transport food around the globe does not reflect the environmental damage that it causes.

- Should the cost of fuel be increased to reflect the cost of putting right the damage it causes?
- Should all foods be taxed proportionately to the distance they travel – from where they are produced to where they are sold?
- Should crops be produced where the conditions for them are most suitable and then transported to where they are sold?

▼ Flying food products by air uses nearly 40 times more fuel than sea transport, but it is now a regular feature of world trade.

▲ Wheat – one of the world's staple foodstuffs – is grown across large areas of the prairies in North America and Canada.

Staple foods

The basic foodstuffs that people rely on are known as staple foods. These are usually low-cost, high-energy foods made from cereals like wheat, rice or maize, vegetables such as potatoes, and pulses such as lentils. These products are usually used to manufacture other foods. For example, wheat is used to make flour, which is then used in many breads, pastries and cakes, while maize is the main ingredient of a tortilla, a popular wrap eaten in central America. Some cereals are also used as animal feed. Staples normally store well and can be transported in bulk easily and cheaply by train, barge or ship.

These basic foodstuffs are needed in vast quantities and global commodity markets have developed for many of them, including wheat, maize, sugar, coffee, tea and cocoa. In some countries large areas of land are devoted to

their cultivation. For example, wheat is grown over vast tracts of prairies in North America and steppes in Russia. When you buy a loaf of bread the wheat from which it is made could have come from any of the wheat-producing countries. The label on a product may just read 'Produce of more than one country'. However, manufacturers normally keep a note of the origin in case there are any health and safety problems for people eating their food.

Country	Production in million tonnes (2005)
China	96
India	72
United States	57
Russian Federation	46
France	37
World	**626**

▲ This table shows the countries that produce the most wheat.

Supply and demand

Prices on the commodity markets determine how much income the farmer receives. Production fluctuates because the weather conditions can change from year to year and from place to place. When the demand for the food is greater than the supply from farmers, the prices are higher and the farmer can do well. When the supply is greater than the demand, the farmer may be forced to sell the produce at a low price, sometimes less than the cost of producing it. The worst situation for a farmer is when his or her production is low due to local conditions, but globally production is very high and so the price is low, too. Some governments try to protect their farmers from such price variations through subsidies, tariffs and other mechanisms (see page 14).

Focus on...
Monitoring food production

Providing food for more than six billion people is a challenge because local weather conditions vary from year to year. It is important to know if there are likely to be surpluses or shortages locally or globally. The US Agency for International Development (USAID) runs the Famine Early Warning System (FEWS), which monitors drought-prone countries in sub-Saharan Africa. Satellites monitor growing conditions and identify areas at risk. Food relief can then be sent to those places in advance. FEWS was established after the 1984 Ethiopian famine, which most of the world learned about only when thousands of people were already starving.

▼ Food aid can be supplied from and to many nations and for different reasons – to help people affected by famine or those who have been driven out of their countries by war. Here, Red Cross workers from Chad assist refugees from Sudan.

Globalisation and Free Trade

Free trade – where there are no tariffs or other barriers to the exchange of goods and services between nations – is considered necessary if the global economy is to benefit from globalisation. However, at a national level, governments consider that free trade in agricultural products can seriously damage national interests, and as a result they have set up many kinds of barriers. Finding acceptable solutions to the problems caused by free trade is proving very difficult.

Early trade

Humans have a very long history of trading artefacts, food and services. At first, trade in food products was very local, taking place in a village or town marketplace. Much the same practice is evident in many LEDCs today. Trade in spices is one of the oldest examples of trading foods over long distances. Spices were highly valued and used in many kinds of rituals. Four hundred years ago the spice trade was the most lucrative in the world, and the desire to control it and profit from it led several European nations to fight each other.

Merchants saw opportunities to exploit areas they were discovering in the New World and Africa. The slave trade between Europe, Africa and the Americas developed so that agricultural products like sugar could be grown on plantations and sold at a huge profit in Europe. Only products that would not deteriorate on a long sea journey could be traded, though.

The expansion of trade

Much of the trade in food products was allowed to proceed unhindered as long as the taxes levied by governments were paid. Most

▲ Spices like these, at a spice market in Egypt, were once a valuable commodity and are still traded between East and West.

▲ During the Second World War many countries, including the United States, had to introduce rationing to ensure that food supplies did not run out. People were issued with coupons to buy certain foods.

of these products were luxury items that had little impact on general farming, which continued to supply most of the basic food needed locally.

However, the trade gradually expanded to include some basic food products. As the population of Europe grew, North America started to export wheat. By the beginning of the twentieth century, European countries had become quite dependent on imports of food. So much so that at the start of the Second World War in 1939, when trade became severely disrupted, it was difficult to feed everyone and rationing had to be introduced.

Focus on...
World trade blocs

Today the world is divided into trade blocs – groups of countries that have negotiated trade agreements between themselves. They play a central role in international trade negotiations. If world trade talks fail, many believe these groups will determine which countries trade with each other and how. The blocs are:

- The Asia-Pacific Economic Co-operation Forum (APEC)
- Cairns Group (a grouping of countries exporting agricultural produce)
- European Union (EU)
- G20 (a grouping of important developing countries)
- North American Free Trade Agreement (NAFTA – controls trade between Canada, the United States and Mexico)

Supporting farmers

The Second World War disrupted trade so much that governments decided their countries should be able to feed themselves in times of emergency, and put systems in place to limit free trade. Farmers in MEDCs were given money and advice to expand the production of basic foodstuffs. In poorer countries, imports of cheap foods were restricted to make sure local farmers did not have to compete with very low prices when selling their produce.

The types of incentives and barriers still used to obstruct free trade are listed below.

Tariffs

When a food product is imported, a tariff is paid to the government. This raises the price of the product, making the local product more competitive.

Quotas

It is difficult for a densely populated country to grow all the basic foodstuffs it needs, so import quotas are set for individual foods. The quota allows the import of an agreed number of tonnes per year to make up for what local farmers cannot produce.

Guaranteed prices

The farmer is told what price will be received for his or her farm produce. The farmer can then plan how much can be spent on production.

Subsidies

The government supplements a farmer's income for growing specific crops to help increase the supply of locally produced food.

Grants and low-cost loans

Farmers are provided with assistance to drain land, buy fertilisers, enlarge fields, fill ponds, buy fences, install irrigation and buy machinery. These help to reduce farming costs. Grants can also be paid for conservation activities on farms.

Free services

The government provides or helps other organisations to provide free research and advice to assist farmers in improving their productivity.

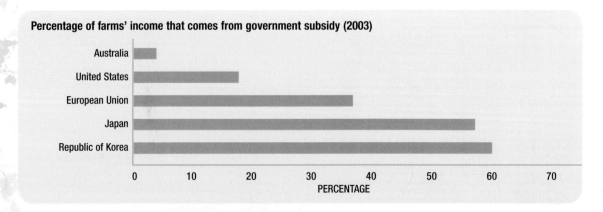

Percentage of farms' income that comes from government subsidy (2003)

▲ Although America is often criticised for the level of subsidies paid to its farmers, it is a lower proportion of a farmer's income than in the European Union or Japan.

The effects of incentives

Support can help farmers increase the yields of most crops and animal products. In some cases huge surpluses of food are created. Some are stored but others are put on the world market in such large quantities that prices fall. Farmers in countries that do not receive subsidies are not able to sell their produce at these prices and make a profit, forcing them to give up or go into debt.

▼ In some MEDCs, incentives can result in huge surpluses of certain foodstuffs being created. This can cause world prices to plummet and in some cases the food is simply dumped because it cannot be sold.

The world is still living with this legacy and vested-interest groups that benefit from these arrangements are fighting against the introduction of free trade in agricultural goods. Most of these groups want the benefits of being able to sell their own produce wherever they want, but want goods competing with theirs excluded from their home markets.

Eyewitness

'America's family farmers and ranchers should not have to compete with cheap, lower-quality imports from countries that pay little or no attention to environmental and labor standards.'
American National Farmers Union

▲ Those who argue against free trade say that large areas of land used for cash crops, like this vineyard in Australia, result in a loss of habitat for wildlife and plants.

Fighting for free trade

Those who want free trade in agricultural goods believe the advantages will be:

Cheaper food

Farmers with the lowest costs will be able to sell their produce anywhere, and the biggest beneficiaries will be poor people who normally spend up to 70 per cent of their income on food.

Greater choice

With open markets, people will be able to enjoy foods that are out of season at home or that cannot be produced locally because the soil or climate conditions are not suitable.

Greater food security

The amount of food harvested in any area can vary by as much as 25 per cent a year depending on the weather. However, over the globe as a whole, production fluctuates very little. Food can be brought in from wherever it is in surplus.

Larger markets, less poverty

Farmers will no longer be dependent on selling their produce locally. One potential benefit is that they will be able to expand production and sell on the world market.

Reducing hunger

Multinational companies could provide advice and support to farmers to help them improve production and cope with difficult growing conditions using new genetically modified (GM) seeds.

Protection of the environment

By increasing productivity on good farmland, there will be less need to use land that is not really suited for agricultural use.

Focus on...
The World Trade Organisation

The World Trade Organisation (WTO) sets the rules for international trade. It was established in 1995, although the General Agreement on Tariffs and Trade (GATT) has been making international trade rules since 1948. National governments are the members of the WTO, and they work through the organisation to make trade between countries easier. Once rules are agreed they are binding, and the WTO deals with any complaints from countries that believe the rules are not being followed.

Fighting against free trade

There are others who believe free trade can harm farmers and the environment in both LEDCs and MEDCs. They believe the disadvantages are:

Increasing poverty

In LEDCs, food markets will be swamped with low-cost produce from overseas, putting local farmers out of business and increasing poverty. Farmers that try to compete may have to borrow money to buy machinery, seeds and chemicals.

Damaging the environment

The new strains of seeds often need more resources like water and chemicals if they are to thrive where growing conditions are not ideal. Normally, farmers use seeds that have been bred over centuries to grow successfully in the local conditions. Also, increasing the transport of produce requires the use of more fuel and thus adds to global warming.

Free trade works against small farms

Small farms cannot compete with the low prices from large farms, often controlled by large companies. As a result, farming cannot normally provide enough income for the family. Small farmers depend on their subsidies to make a decent living. If these are removed, they can go out of business and large companies will buy the land to create huge farms.

Loss of biodiversity

Modern farming methods used on ever-larger farms provide less room for wildlife. Mixed farming provides more habitats for wildlife than the monocultures that are often a feature of large farms. One of the claims of organic farmers is that organic farming is better for wildlife. The International Federation of

Organic Agriculture Movements (IFOAM) is an international agricultural association that supports farming based on organic farming principles. However, the big GM seed producers like Monsanto also claim that using their seeds can benefit wildlife.

▲ These people are demonstrating against the WTO during a meeting of the organisation in Hong Kong.

Have your say

Politicians agree the rules about trade in foodstuffs through the WTO. National governments have to make sure the rules are followed or penalties are enforced. The WTO is not a democratic organisation, and citizens of individual countries have no way of changing the rules made by the WTO.

- If you felt strongly that a WTO rule was wrong, what could you do about it?
- What kind of information should be included on food packaging to help consumers decide whether or not to buy it?
- Is there any issue that you feel so strongly about that once all peaceful methods had been exhausted, you might consider non-peaceful action?

Food Producers Around the World

Farmers make up only one group involved in food production, and there are many others. These include seed producers, agricultural chemicals companies, merchants, agricultural machine manufacturers and engineers, agricultural researchers, water engineers, food-processing companies, hauliers, wholesalers, supermarkets and food chains.

Making informed choices

As many as 60 companies might be involved in making one tin of chicken noodle soup. Each group is trying to make as much money as it can, but while they all have a common interest in food and farming, they have different ideas about how farming should be carried out. At the end of this long chain is you – the consumer. Ultimately, millions of individual choices will govern how agriculture is run. For example, if

consumers decide not to buy any foods that have genetically modified ingredients, then there is no point in farmers producing them. With good information, people are able to make choices about the types of food they wish to eat. Obtaining this information can be difficult because much of that currently available is biased. It comes from vested-interest groups such as seed producers, campaign groups, the supermarkets or food chains like Burger King.

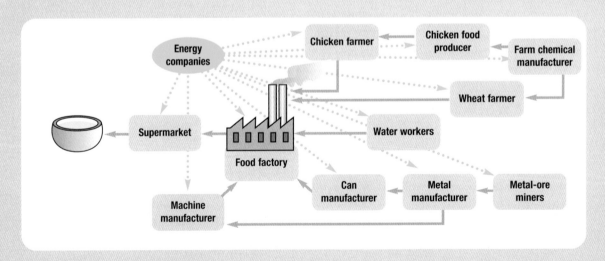

▲ There are usually several groups of people involved in the creation and distribution of a single food item. This diagram shows who might play a part in the process of producing a tin of chicken noodle soup.

▲ A farmer ploughs a field outside the village of Tadecha Gurach in Ethiopia. This area is extremely dry and local people have started a co-operative to improve irrigation.

Farming for the future

Most of the big international companies producing seeds, chemicals for controlling weeds, pests and diseases, fertilisers and agricultural machinery support globalisation because it increases their potential market. However, farmers and governments differ in their viewpoints. Some support and others object to globalisation.

At the heart of the globalisation conflict in agriculture is the fact that, for many people, farming is more than just growing food. It is a way of life, and is largely responsible for the appearance of the rural landscape and the wildlife that exists there. Farmland is often passed from one generation to the next, each one wishing to protect the land for the future.

Most people living in towns in MEDCs have a romantic view of what the countryside should be like and generally favour the type of landscape created by small mixed farms.

Owners of small farms fear that free trade in farm produce favours large farms specialising in one or two products. These will cause small farms to become uneconomic, making a way of life extinct and creating new, more monotonous landscapes.

Focus on...
Co-operatives

Small farms growing cash crops like coffee alongside their food crops can compete with the big producers if they work together as a co-operative. One such organisation is the Oromia Coffee Farmers Co-operative Union of Ethiopia, which represents 115 local co-operatives. Over 600,000 households in this region produce two-thirds of Ethiopia's coffee. The Union is responsible for selling the coffee they produce, and 70 per cent of the profits go back to the co-operatives, which then distribute the income to the households. Farmers choose to sell through the Union because they like the security and advantages it offers.

Buy local or global?

There are many environmental groups that also warn of the dangers of globalisation and free trade in farm produce. They believe that modern farming methods, while producing cheaper food, have a damaging impact on wildlife, the rural landscape and rural communities. With fewer jobs in the countryside, people have to find work in towns. Villages become too small to support a shop, a bus service, a school or health centre.

Environmental groups often recommend that people should buy locally produced food, farmed in ways that do not harm wildlife or the appearance of the landscape. In particular, pressure groups have highlighted the treatment of animals on farms and have suggested that organisations like the WTO should be taking animal welfare more seriously when considering their policies.

No easy solutions

Government support for farmers has been seen as a way of protecting rural communities and the character of the countryside, as well as ensuring there is food to eat. But the same protection offered to small farms is also available to the big farms. They can become even more profitable and buy up the small farms the subsidies were designed to protect.

Subsidies mean that produce can be sold at a lower price than non-subsidised farmers in other countries can produce it. For example, rice farmers in the United States receive subsidies. Rice farmers in Asia are worried that if tariff barriers on rice imported from the United States are removed, they will not be able to compete with a flood of subsidised rice from America. However, the government

▲ A rice farmer in the United States checks his crop. The farmers who do best from farm subsidies in the United States are those with large farms. Twenty per cent of farms are mainly small farms and they receive only 10 per cent of the subsidies paid by the government.

of the United States then threatens to impose tariff barriers on industrial products being exported to the United States from countries in Asia.

There are other pressure groups that say the rich countries should remove support for their own agriculture so that farmers in LEDCs can compete with them on equal terms. In such countries, where governments cannot afford to subsidise farmers, prices at the market are low because produce that is surplus to requirements in the subsidised countries is sold at low prices. Dumping undermines local markets and free trade.

Focus on...
Animal welfare

The rules of the WTO make it difficult for countries to make life better for farm animals. A country cannot prevent animal products being imported simply because they do not approve of the farming methods. For example, the European Union has banned keeping hens in battery cages from 2012. However, it will be against WTO rules for the EU to ban the import of eggs from battery hens in countries outside the EU. As these are likely to be cheaper, egg farmers in the EU may have to close down.

▼ Persuading people in Europe to buy eggs only from humanely managed hens rather than those raised on battery farms is not against the trade rules. It is up to consumers to make the choice.

The power of multinational food and farming companies

World trade in farm products can encourage producers to expand into areas that previously were not farmed. For example, the Amazon rainforest has suffered with the expansion of farming soya beans, which are mainly used to make feed for animals in Europe. Large food companies like McDonald's were selling chicken that had been fed on soya from the Amazon. Greenpeace mounted a campaign to persuade customers to contact the European headquarters of the company to protest. McDonald's, along with some other major retailers, has now agreed to stop using soya from newly felled areas of the Amazon. This is putting pressure on the big five soya trading companies to negotiate how best to protect areas like the Amazon rainforest.

Although multinational companies have a lot of power, they need to protect their image if they are to enjoy continued success. Pressure groups like Greenpeace can help focus on particular issues or companies, but in the end it is consumers that make the difference.

Palm plantations

Soya is not the only agricultural product causing destruction of the rainforest. One in 10 foods contains palm oil, and to satisfy the demand for this, large areas of forest in Southeast Asia have been cleared to make way

▼ Police stand guard outside a McDonald's restaurant in the United Kingdom. The fast-food chain has been subject to much criticism, and sometimes violent attacks, because of its policies.

for oil-palm plantations. Multinational food companies like Unilever have led the expansion of palm-oil production. In Malaysia, oil-palm plantations cover 40 per cent of the cultivated land and production is growing in Indonesia, the Philippines and Thailand, amongst others. It is big business and provides these countries with income. This makes it very difficult for those arguing the case for conservation. Company brochures do not mention the declining number of orang-utans, among our closest relatives in the rest of the animal kingdom, or the extinction of many other species of plants and animals that results from the clearing of land for this use. There is increasing pressure on the big supermarkets from their customers to show

that they purchase their foods responsibly, not just cheaply. Major producers like Unilever are now working on making production more sustainable. The situation could become worse if there is a growth in the use of biofuels, as palm oil would be a major source of the fuel.

Eyewitness

'Decisions about how our food is grown and by whom are made behind closed doors. Trade and agricultural ministers have allowed multinational corporations to gain unprecedented power and control over our food system.'
UK aid organisation FoodAid

▼ High oil prices and a recent demand for renewable energy have boosted the development of alternative fuels such as palm oil, which is extracted from palm fruits like these on a plantation in Malaysia.

Food for the Global Market

International trade in food has grown by more than 400 per cent over the last 40 years and is set to expand further. What foods are being traded and does the food trade resolve as many issues as it creates?

Global trade in food products is divided into a number of categories. There are commodities – these are mainly unprocessed foods that can be bought and sold by traders around the world. They include coffee, sugar, cocoa, maize, soya beans, soya-bean meal, wheat, sunflower oil, linseed oil, soya oil, orange juice as well as some meat. Other foods that are traded include fresh ones like milk, fruit and vegetables, and processed foods like butter and cheese.

Commodities

Commodities are traded internationally but the traders may never see what they buy. Take sugar as an example. Typically a trader will buy an agreed quantity at the sugar market in London or New York. Once the trader becomes the owner, he or she can then sell the sugar on to another trader or a food producer. Sometimes traders promise to buy an agreed amount of sugar before it has been harvested. This is called the futures market. Later, if sugar is in short supply, the traders

▼ Commodities are traded on commodity markets. Traders buy up quantities of a product – sometimes before it has even been produced – and sell it later, hoping that its value will have increased.

▲ In countries like Colombia small shops once dominated. Now more than half of food sales here comes from supermarkets.

will be able to sell their sugar at a much higher price than they bought it for.

The prices that farmers receive depend on the quality of the crop and the amounts available for sale. If the total quantity produced worldwide exceeds the demand, the price will be lower than if there is a shortage. With commodities, a farmer has to compete with farmers from other countries. Those who can produce at the lowest cost are likely to make the most profit. The lowest-cost producers are usually those with huge farms that use lots of machinery.

Once a commodity is processed it can be sold at a much higher price. The farmer gets only a small proportion of the price that you might pay for a food product in the shop. For example, if a chocolate bar costs 100 units in a shop, then 28 units will be taken by the shop, 40 units by the company making the

bar and only seven go to the farmer. The rest goes in taxes. Ideally, the country in which the cocoa beans were produced would also process them into chocolate bars. However, importing countries sometimes create tariff barriers for processed foods so they can protect their own companies.

Focus on...
Supermarkets and food

More and more people are buying their food from big supermarket chains. In South America and East Asia, where small family food shops and market stalls once dominated sales, the supermarket share of food sales has ballooned from less than 20 per cent to more than 50 per cent over the past decade. The biggest supermarkets, mainly owned by giant multinational companies, control 65 to 95 per cent of all supermarket sales in Latin America. Increasingly, supermarkets are dealing direct with farmers around the world to stock their shelves.

▲ Large plantations for crops such as tea can help the economies of LEDCs, but they also take up large areas and local farmers can be removed from their land.

Plantation agriculture

Many of the agricultural commodities grown in tropical countries are raised on plantations. Plantations are usually developed and run by commercial companies, large landowners, governments or a combination of these. The aim is to use the natural amenable conditions for that crop to earn money from exports to the global market. The country can use the income to pay for development programmes such as healthcare, road building and education. Examples of crops grown for food on plantations are sugar, bananas, oil palm, coffee, tea and coconuts.

Plantations can have some damaging impacts, too. They cover large areas and replace the native plants and animals. Also, local people, including farmers, may be moved off the land with little or no compensation to make way for the plantations. They may have no other choice but to become a labourer on the plantation, often receiving very low wages.

The dangers of specialisation

Many LEDCs receive a large part of their income from exports from a few agricultural commodities. For example, St Kitts and Nevis in the Caribbean earns 94 per cent of its agricultural exports from sugar. Such countries compete against one another to sell their produce on the world market. According to the United Nations, 43 LEDCs rely on just one commodity for more than a fifth of all their income from exports. Most of these countries are in sub-Saharan Africa, Latin America and the Caribbean, and they depend on exports of coffee, bananas, cotton lint or cocoa beans. Prices for these commodities go up and down each year, but over the last 20 years they have fallen overall. Meanwhile, prices for imports such as machinery and farm chemicals have generally increased. The countries are earning less from exports but paying more for imports. They cannot afford to spend money on equipment and new techniques to make production more efficient, or diversify into other products. The countries are trapped in poverty. Globalisation is a problem for them.

Processed foods

Food-processing companies often deal directly with farmers in the countries where they operate. The companies want to make sure that the quality of food they receive is up to standard and at a price agreed with the farmer in advance. Often, the companies dictate precisely how the crops should be grown or animals reared. Having a contract with a major food producer can be a mixed blessing. On one hand farmers have the security of knowing that they can sell their crop at a fixed price. On the other hand the weather may be bad and the crop may not

reach the standard required, in which case other buyers have to be found. Also, farmers may gear their farm to the requirements of the food-processing company. They are then not in a good position to negotiate with the company should it want to reduce the price or offer the contract to other farmers, maybe in a different part of the world where costs are lower.

Focus on...
Monoculture

Monoculture is a farming system where only one crop is grown. Huge banana, sugar, oil-palm and tea plantations established in tropical countries are examples of monocultures. In temperate areas too, farmers may specialise in one crop, such as the large wheat farms found in the Canadian prairie provinces. Globalisation favours monocultures because they make production, marketing and transport much easier and therefore cheaper.

▼ These workers in a food-processing factory are checking chicken for food-safety standards.

Fresh foods

Fresh foods need to reach shops quickly before they deteriorate. If they are produced for a local market this is not a problem. However, many fresh foods are seasonal and have to be carried long distances to keep shops supplied all year round. Refrigerated lorries carry produce from the southern states of America to the north in winter. The same happens in Europe, with lorry loads of salad crops travelling from Spain to northern Europe. Some higher-value foods travel even further and come by air. Excessive use of transport, especially air travel, contributes to global warming. This is one of the undesirable impacts of globalisation in the food industry.

Large supermarkets also save money by having central distribution depots for their foods. All foods are brought to the depots. There the orders for individual sites are collected, loaded on to a lorry and taken to the shop. Without the consumer realising, the lettuce they buy may have been produced on a farm close by, but then transported to a distant distribution depot – then back to the shop.

Local produce for local markets

People are increasingly being asked to buy local produce to try to reduce the distance travelled by food before it is eaten. Local food is becoming increasingly popular, and to fill the

Eyewitness

'Small farms are increasingly concerned at the power of supermarkets to squeeze them on price, often forcing them to take prices lower than production costs.'
Claudius Jan-Marie, a banana farmer in St Lucia

▼ Central distribution depots are used by many big supermarkets. All the food they sell is brought here – even if it is then transported back to a store near where it was produced.

demand, farmers are setting up farmers' markets. These markets are held regularly in towns and villages. Farmers can sell their produce direct to customers. Customers can talk to the farmer about how the food is produced and can be assured that it has only travelled from the farm to the market.

The role of subsidies

Government payments to farmers in more developed parts of the world, such as Europe and North America, often dictate what the farmers produce and how. The payments are normally made to help farmers increase production of particular crops like rice or wheat, or animal products such as meat. These subsidies hinder free trade in food and have led to surpluses of some foods. Subsidies have also encouraged intensive use of the land, causing environmental damage. New Zealand has already removed most forms of subsidies, and the European Union is changing how it supports farmers. Instead of paying farmers subsidies for producing a particular product, they are to be paid for farming the land in environmentally friendly ways.

Focus on...
Australia – almost a subsidy-free zone

Australian farmers receive almost no subsidies. Just four per cent of their income comes from government support. In 2003, Warren Truss, a minister in the Australian government, said that Australia's experience of scrapping farm subsidies had helped it become one of the most efficient farming nations in the world. Australia leads the Cairns Group, an international organisation of major farm-produce exporters that includes Argentina, Brazil, Canada, Indonesia, Malaysia, New Zealand and South Africa. The group works to end farm subsidies in all countries.

▲ More and more people are buying their food from farmers markets, where they can discuss the product with the people who have grown it.

Can Free Trade be Fair Trade?

There are those who say the fairest trade of all is free trade. If there are no barriers to trade, then everyone has an equal chance of success. There are others who argue that free trade can never be fair because there have to be rules and these will always be set by the most powerful groups. Who should we believe?

The agribusiness agenda

Corporations have a duty to their shareholders. Their duty is to protect the shareholders' investment in the company and generate income for them. Although they have to abide by the law, farm companies are not in business to protect rural jobs, ways of life, biodiversity or to feed the world, unless that is what generates the best return for shareholders. They support globalisation and free trade because it will enable them to grow and make more money for their shareholders.

Several organisations are concerned that the livelihoods of many farmers are being undermined, that the environment is being damaged and biodiversity is being reduced by the expansion of globalisation and free trade. They are concerned that a global uniformity of farming will replace thousands of local farming systems that have adapted to local climate and soil conditions over centuries.

Before accepting what any pressure group has to say, it is important to consider why they hold that point of view. This is as true for those who campaign against globalisation and free trade as those campaigning for them.

Who is likely to benefit and who is likely to lose from them getting their way? Are their suggested methods sustainable? Can the activity produce the food that is needed, at a price people can afford, while protecting the environment on which all farming depends? Can they protect the societies in which we live while keeping shareholders happy? Are there any other systems that could work better? These are all significant questions that have caused great debate.

▲ Agribusinesses use a lot of machinery, which reduces the need for workers on farms. People against large-scale agribusiness believe that smaller farms and more traditional methods are better for local economies and the environment.

▲ These workers are picking coffee beans on a farm in Ethiopia. The farm is a Fair Trade operation, which means that these workers will receive a fair price for their coffee beans.

The Fair Trade alternative

An alternative global movement is known as Fair Trade. Fair Trade is a growing worldwide movement that makes sure farmers in poor countries get a good deal. They are given a fair price for their goods (one that covers the cost of production and guarantees a sustainable living). They also have long-term contracts so they can enjoy security from year to year. Farmers are also taught the skills they need for their business and are encouraged to practise more organic and sustainable methods of production. Although small in total amount of agricultural goods traded, the movement has attracted the imaginations of companies and customers alike. Most supermarkets stock some Fair Trade products.

A drawback of guaranteeing a price for what a farmer produces is that there may be no incentive to improve the quality of the produce. There has to be a demand for Fair Trade products in order to justify supply. If the quality is not good, then the demand will decrease and farmers will find they are unable to sell all their produce.

Have your say

The idea of Fair Trade is undoubtedly a good one, but while it can have positive effects for farmers in LEDCs, there are drawbacks, too, and many people do not fully understand what Fair Trade actually means.

- How might general knowledge about Fair Trade be improved?
- Would you buy Fair Trade products, even though they cost a bit more?
- Is it right for organisations to interfere with the farming strategies of other countries, even if their intentions are good?

Fixed payments

The Fair Trade movement began with development agencies working mainly in LEDCs agreeing to pay farmers a guaranteed price for their produce, whatever the world market price was. Before this, farmers had to sell their crops at prices that varied from year to year. Sometimes they received less than it cost to produce their crop. With no guarantee of a reasonable income, it was difficult for farmers to plan how much to invest in their farm.

The first Fair Trade label was launched in 1986 on coffee from Mexico. Since then the movement has grown. In 2005, trade in Fair Trade goods was over US$1 billion. Many types of goods are traded, but the two most common are bananas and coffee.

Conning the consumer?

Café Direct is a global business selling teas, chocolate and coffee. It is committed to Fair Trade. It pays farmers a guaranteed price that is higher than they are likely to get on the world market. Farmers can expect to double their income from coffee. The coffee is sold in shops and some coffee chains. Although the amount paid to the farmer is much higher, when you buy a cup of Fair Trade coffee, it will cost the seller less than one extra penny a cup. This is because the cost of the coffee in the cup is a very small part of the price you pay. Vendors selling Fair Trade cups of coffee at a higher price than ordinary coffee are usually exploiting their customers and making more profit.

The term 'Fair Trade' refers to an idea that is accepted by the wider Fair Trade movement. The term 'Fairtrade' refers to the specific labelling system controlled by Fairtrade

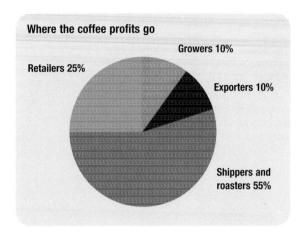

Where the coffee profits go

Growers 10%

Retailers 25%

Exporters 10%

Shippers and roasters 55%

▲ The majority of the profit from coffee sales goes to the large corporations that control most of the coffee market. The coffee producers only receive 10 per cent of the profits.

Labelling Organisations International (FLO) and its member organisations. This sets standards and monitors them. The quantities of Fair Trade produce bought in MEDCs is growing rapidly. In Europe, five per cent of the coffee sold is Fair Trade. In Switzerland, 25 per cent of bananas sold are Fair Trade. In the United Kingdom, about US$69 million of Fair Trade products are sold. In the United States growth has been slower, but one company, Equal Exchange, saw its sales increase 34 per cent in a single year and is expanding its product lines. It also has a distribution agreement with United Natural Foods and has expanded into such mainstream supermarkets as Safeway, Albertsons and Shaw's.

Consumer power

Many people are concerned about modern farming, wherever it takes place. However, they do not always share the same concerns. A survey in 2006 by the International Food Information Council found that Americans were largely unconcerned about biotechnology and the use of it in farming.

In Europe, more people are concerned about biotechnology. In the press, foods produced in this way are often referred to as 'Frankenstein foods'. Public opinion has played a major role in persuading Europe to reject genetically modified foods until more research has been carried out.

But what influences public opinion? While information based on sound science is generally accepted as the best method of reaching an informed decision, most people rely on what is provided by the media, the government and the many pressure groups wanting to promote a particular viewpoint. When choosing what to believe, it is important to see where the information originated and then consider what their interest is.

▼ Fair Trade coffee is now big business, and many companies in MEDCs support Fair Trade operations around the world.

Eyewitness

According to a poll conducted by the European Commission, Europeans are more likely than Americans...

'...to view agricultural biotech [modifying plants and animals to have certain characteristics] as a threat … to the moral order, and more likely to associate biotech foods with menacing images of adulteration, infection and monsters.'

Focus on...
Fairtrade

Globally, an estimated five million people – farmers, workers and their families – are already benefiting from the Fairtrade system. Fairtrade is currently working in 58 developing countries, with 464 producer organisations and 515 registered traders.

The organic alternative

Another reaction to the WTO brand of globalisation has been the growth of an international organic farming movement. Organic farming is different from other modern commercial agricultural systems in that it avoids using artificial chemicals. It uses alternative ways of controlling pests and diseases, and providing crops with sufficient nutrients to grow strongly. Farmers try to imitate rather than replace natural systems. For example, by ensuring a farm is rich in insects, pests can be controlled by their natural predators. Leaving hedges and wild spaces on a farm helps maintain a variety of insects. Weeds are controlled by digging them up or by mulching – a technique that insulates the soil by covering it with organic material like straw, vegetable waste or bark chippings. The fertility of the soil is maintained by rotating crops grown on a piece of land each year and using manure. Organic farmers also use naturally occurring fertilisers such as rock phosphate and potash.

Organic farms that raise livestock and poultry provide animals with more natural living conditions and feed them on foods that have been grown organically. Crowding, often responsible for the spread of diseases like foot and mouth or bird flu, becomes less widespread.

Setting organic standards

It is important that people who wish to buy organic produce know that it has been produced to organic standards. Many countries have national bodies that certify

▼ A worker checks on green beans grown in an organic garden in the United Kingdom.

farm products produced to their organic standards. However, there is now an international trade in organic produce similar to that in conventional farm produce. Customers need to be confident that when they are buying organic produce, they know what organic means. The International Federation of Organic Agriculture Movements (IFOAM) is an international agricultural association that is working towards the 'adoption of ecologically, socially and economically sound systems that are based on the principles of Organic Agriculture'. IFOAM has developed an organic farming standard and a system for awarding organic certificates for produce.

The economic advantages of organic cultivation

Organic farming is providing a profitable alternative to some farmers, who could not compete on price with produce from elsewhere. For example, Indonesia has a tradition of rice farming, with thousands of small family farms producing rice for the family and a surplus to sell at local markets. Globalisation agreements have meant that restrictions on imported rice have been eased. Local farmers have found they cannot compete on price with cheaper imports, often grown by big overseas producers. Many have moved to organic methods of cultivation.

Rice grown organically receives a higher price in the market. Organic farmers normally use local varieties of rice that are better suited to the local conditions, have a better taste and have a longer shelf life than the high-yielding hybrid varieties. In addition, many farmers also cultivate fish along with the rice crop, providing farmers with another source of food and income. The fish can survive because there are no damaging artificial chemicals being used that could poison them.

The global market for organic products was worth US$25.5 billion in 2005, with the vast majority of products being consumed in North America and Europe.

▲ Thanks to the growth of the organic movement, rice grown in paddy fields, planted and harvested using traditional methods, is now popular and can command a higher price in the market, improving the situation for rice farmers.

Have your say

It is not always possible to buy all organic ingredients needed for a particular dish, such as a vegetable curry. If you are preparing a dish at home, you can choose to include non-organic ingredients. Food manufacturers face the same problem.

- If they include some non-organic ingredients, should they be able to label the product as 'organic'?
- Would you give a different answer if the proportion of organic ingredients by weight was 95 per cent, 75 per cent or 50 per cent of the total?
- What if it was only the spices in the curry that were non-organic?

The Future of Farming

In the next 30 years or so the global population could reach 12 billion. Will free trade and new farming technologies provide the means of feeding everyone? What might farming in the future be like?

Food security

A major concern of many LEDCs about free trade in agricultural produce is that the state will not be able to fulfil one of its key responsibilities – ensuring its citizens are adequately fed. Article 25 of the Universal Declaration of Human Rights states: 'Everyone has the right to a standard of living adequate for the health and well-being of himself and of his family, including food'.

Many countries are already failing to provide their populations with secure food supplies.

▲ Wheat is loaded on to a cargo ship in Canada, ready to be transported all over the world. Globalisation has allowed food to be carried to many of the countries that might need it most.

The Food and Agricultural Organisation estimates that about 842 million people in the world are undernourished and of these, almost 800 million live in LEDCs. Every day 25,000 people die of hunger or a hunger-related condition. Will globalisation help or hinder the process of providing sufficient food for everyone?

Despite all the claims of the benefits of globalisation, many areas of the world still have millions of people that are undernourished.

Is globalisation helping?

Those who believe globalisation is helping offer the following reasons:

● Globalisation is already ensuring emergency food aid can be delivered to areas where food shortages are likely or are actually happening. Surpluses, mainly produced in MEDCs, are held in stores and made available as necessary.
● Countries will be able to specialise in those food products that the climate and soil conditions favour and export to other countries. With the money earned they can buy food.

Region	1990–92	1995–97	2002–04
Sub-Saharan Africa	164	180	213
Near East and North Africa	26	33	37
East and Southeast Asia	283	241	227
South Asia	299	284	300
Latin America and the Caribbean	59	53	52
Industrialised countries	9	8	9
Countries in transition	20	26	23

▲ This table shows the numbers of undernourished people (in millions) in various regions of the world over a period of 15 years.

● Food will be cheaper because it is grown where conditions are best and therefore costs are lowest. Food will be more affordable for poorer people.

There is also a strong anti-globalisation movement, which thinks globalisation is part of the problem rather than the solution to feeding the world's population. These groups usually prefer to encourage local farmers to produce food for local markets and to ensure that they are paid a fair price. One famous campaigner for fairer rules governing world trade in agricultural goods is José Bové. He was one of the candidates for the French presidency in 2007. One event that brought him to public notice was the dismantling of a McDonald's restaurant in France in 1999. He wanted to raise awareness about McDonald's importing hormone-treated beef, which he opposed. Bové was sentenced to three months in prison for this.

In reality, there is no single way of guaranteeing there is sufficient food for everyone. All actions have some undesirable consequences. Globalisation favours big producers and multinationals at the expense of small farmers. Relying on local farmers for our food supply could mean starvation when a harvest fails. Finding fair solutions to these very complex issues is not easy because there are so many competing interests to be satisfied. People vote for politicians to consider the issues and make decisions.

▲ Globalisation in food and farming can help small farmers and their local communities, allowing them to be globally competitive.

37

▲ This anti-GM food protester is pulling up genetically modified crops. Such campaigners believe that genetic modification is wrong because no one is sure what the long-term consequences might be.

Biotechnology – friend or foe?

Farmers and seed producers have been breeding different varieties of the same plant and animal species for centuries. In plant breeding they select seeds from plants that have shown a particular characteristic – for example, wheat that managed to survive through a drought. They then grow these seeds in dry conditions and select the best of those to breed. Gradually they create a new variety of wheat that is able to grow in areas with low rainfall. They can breed plants to be more resistant to pests and diseases, more productive or more suitable for local conditions. Modern varieties of seeds are good food producers and have been responsible for dramatic increases in the amount of food available. Animals can be selectively bred in the same way, for example, to be good milk producers.

Today, scientists are able to take the genes from one species of plant or animal and combine them with the genes of another. This is known as biotechnology and it could have far-reaching consequences for world farming. The big companies developing this biotechnology say that they can now make plants much more productive and even environmentally friendly, because they can breed them to need fewer chemicals and fertilisers. It will be possible to use new, high-yielding varieties to feed the world. Maize and soya are two GM crops that are regularly grown and most people are happy for them to be in the food they eat. Countries growing GM crops include Argentina, Australia, Bulgaria, Canada, China, Colombia, Germany, Honduras, India, Indonesia, Mexico, Romania, South Africa, Spain, Uruguay and the United States.

Biotechnology sceptics

Some countries and people are sceptical of the claims of the biotechnology companies and a fear that doing something that nature itself seems to have avoided could lead to serious consequences. For example, there is evidence that crops that have been engineered to withstand a certain type of weedkiller pass on characteristics to their wild relatives through cross-pollination. The fear is that 'superweeds' are being created and that they will be difficult to eliminate.

The truth is that research in biotechnology needs to take many years so that the effects on the environment and human health can be monitored. However, companies promoting the technology want returns on the money they have invested more quickly than that.

Eyewitness

Some global technologies, like mobile phones, have brought surprising and unexpected benefits to farmers. Farmers in parts of India are able to subscribe to a text-message service that provides them with weather forecasts and warnings. On the evening of 11 November, grape farmer Arun More received a text message from a laboratory 220 km away at Mumbai. Sent by Agrocom Pvt Ltd, the text message predicted unseasonable rain two days later. And that's exactly what happened:

'Since I had prior information, I could spray fungicide accordingly. I managed to save my orchard from the mildew that would have destroyed the crop.'

▼ This farmer in Kenya is sending a text message to find out about the latest maize prices so she knows what her crop is worth.

▲ Traditional farming methods are changing as small farmers cannot compete with large suppliers. In mountainous areas such as the Alps, many dairy farmers can no longer afford to move their cows to fresh high-altitude pastures in the warm summer months.

Diversity in farming

One major concern of the impact of globalisation on food and farming is that farming will become increasingly uniform. Some people fear that local character in farming will be replaced by a global character of large farms located in depopulated countrysides, specialising in a few products and selling direct to supermarkets and food producers possibly hundreds of kilometres away.

Nature survives by doing the opposite. Evolution leads to diversity. Throughout most of history, farming has been diverse too. Farmers have adapted their techniques to local conditions. They have reared crops and animals that suit those conditions. As a result,

within the global farming community there are many varieties of the same farm crop, all suited to particular environmental conditions. Ways of life evolved around the farm systems. In mountain areas, highland pastures were used in summer for grazing dairy cattle while fields lower down were harvested for hay for winter feed. Many upland pastures have been abandoned, as farmers cannot compete with the large producers of milk. It is cheaper to buy cattle feed than move the cattle around. In Indonesia, terraces were built in hillsides for planting rice. The fields are small and production costs high. It is much cheaper to buy imported rice. Many of the terraces are now abandoned and crumbling, with the resulting danger of soil erosion and flooding from the water that runs down the hills.

Economies of scale

If free trade in farm produce becomes the norm, the current trend to uniformity could accelerate. Economies of scale will favour larger and more specialised farms and small farms will not be able to compete.

Intensive production methods are likely to use fewer varieties or breeds of plants and animals, and many ancient varieties could be lost. In China, of the nearly 10,000 wheat varieties in use in 1949, only 1,000 remained by the 1970s. The United Nations has warned that around 20 per cent of domestic animal breeds are at risk of extinction due to globalisation. Livestock markets favour highly productive breeds over others that, for example, may be better in dry areas or able to graze on unusual food like seaweed. The gene pool that could be important for food security in the future as climate and vegetation change could be lost.

Have your say

Globalisation in food and farming seems to be concentrating responsibility for supplying our food into the hands of fewer and fewer companies. Companies are only accountable to their shareholders, and shareholders are most interested in how much money the company is making for them.

- Is anyone looking after the interests of customers, the farmers, rural communities and the environment?
- Do you think your food is safe in their hands?
- Do you have enough choice in what you buy and how it is produced?
- What messages would you like to send to your government, your local supermarket or the World Trade Organisation?

Focus on...
Sustainable farming

To feed future generations farming needs to be sustainable. Any developments in farming need to be tried and tested to minimise the risk to future production. Sustainable arable farming means:

- Ensuring a secure supply of food for all into the foreseeable future.
- Producing high-yielding, good-quality crops.
- Using as few artificial chemicals and fertilisers as possible.
- Preventing pollution of the air, land and water.
- Conserving local wildlife.
- Conserving local varieties of farm crops.
- Supporting diverse and thriving communities.

▼ Just over 50 years ago there were thousands of varieties of wheat grown in China. Today there is less than 10 per cent of that amount.

The Great Debate

Clearly there are advantages and disadvantages in the changes that globalisation has brought to the food and farming industries. These are summarised below. Remember that many of them are opinions rather than scientifically proven facts, though. Can you tell the difference? In the end, everyone has to make decisions based on some facts, the opinions of others and what they think is right.

Advantages include:

- Globalisation is happening. It is best to use the opportunities it provides and reap the benefits.
- The global food supply will increase.
- Farmers will be able to produce what is best suited to their farmland and sell their produce anywhere.
- For consumers, the price of food should be lower.
- More and better information will allow farmers to increase productivity and profits.
- Surplus food can be stored and distributed to countries where there are shortages.
- Farmers in LEDCs will have better access to the richer markets in MEDCs.
- Land that is not needed for farming can be reforested or restored to its natural state.
- Food produce will be more uniform, making it easier for food manufacturers to maintain a constant quality.

Disadvantages include:

- Food supply in countries could become less secure as farmers specialise in a few cash crops and the country depends more on imported food.
- Globalisation favours the big producers. Small family farms will not be able to compete.
- There will be fewer varieties or breeds of agricultural plants and animals. The gene pool from which new varieties can be bred will be diminished.
- Globalisation favours big farms that provide fewer habitats for wildlife.
- Globalisation favours intensive farming methods. The welfare of farm animals is not a priority.
- Globalisation provides opportunities for a few giant multinational companies to dominate the global supply of food.
- The current vibrant variety of farming methods, landscapes and market systems will be replaced by a standard uniformity.

Facts and Figures

- There are more than six billion people living on Earth at the moment. The population is expected to continue increasing.

- Starbucks is the largest coffee-house company in the world with 13,168 stores in 39 countries (February 2007).

- In five of the last six years, more grains were consumed than farmers produced. The shortfall was made up by using grain held in storage for use in emergency.

- More than 850 million people in the world, including 300 million children go hungry every year.

- A report by Christian Aid estimates that 184 million people in Africa could die before the end of the century from floods, famine, drought and conflict resulting from climate change.

- With some money to buy better seeds, fertilisers, a share in a protected water source, and a bed net to fend off malarial mosquitoes, hundreds of thousands of villagers in the Millennium Villages project in 10 African countries are now able to grow enough food and sell the surplus.

- The top 10 food manufacturers in the world are: Cadbury Schweppes (UK), Coca-Cola (USA), ConAgra (USA), Danone (France), Kraft (USA), Masterfoods/Mars (USA), Nestlé (Switzerland), PepsiCo (USA), Tyson (USA), Unilever (Netherlands/UK).

- The turnover of the American company Wal-Mart is US$256 billion a year, including its food sales.

- Since 1997 more than 25,000 Indian farmers have committed suicide – most attributed to the pressures of corporate globalisation and free-trade policies implemented by the World Trade Organisation.

- The five most heavily traded agricultural products in the world are cereals, sugar, coffee, cocoa and bananas.

Further Information

Books

Food
by Paul Mason (Raintree, 2006)

Food and Farming: Feeding an Expanding World
by Philip Wilkinson (Chrysalis, 2005)

Food: Ethical Debates in What we Eat (Dilemmas in Modern Science)
by Jim Kerr (Evans Brothers, 2008)

Food for All
by Chris Oxlade and Rufus Bellamy (Franklin Watts, 2004)

Food Matters
by Jillian Powell (Evans Brothers, 1999)

From DNA to GM Wheat: Discovering Genetically Modified Food
by John Farndon (Heinemann Library, 2006)

Genetically Modified Food
by Nigel Hawkes (Franklin Watts, 2000)

Websites

www.weforum.org/en/index.htm
The website of the World Economic Forum, with all the latest news on how the problems associated with globalisation are being addressed.

www.foei.org/
Friends of the Earth International, the largest environmental network on the web, with news, campaigns and how to get involved.

www.greenpeace.org/international/
The website of the international charity Greenpeace, which campaigns on environmental issues, including those related to food and farming.

www.monsanto.com/monsanto/layout/default.asp
Monsanto is a multinational agricultural company geared towards helping farmers around the world produce healthier foods in a sustainable way.

www.oxfam.org/
The website for Oxfam International has news about the latest developments and campaigns on humanitarian issues, including fair trade for farmers around the world.

www.fao.org/
The Food and Agricultural Organisation of the United Nations is one of the leading regulatory bodies in food and farming, and its website contains loads of information on all aspects of the subject.

www.wto.org/
The website of the World Trade Organisation, with all the latest news and developments in global trade.

Glossary

biodiversity the variety of plant and animal species within an environment.

biotech modifying plants and animals to have new characteristics for use in farming and food production, for example increasing a plant's immunity to a disease, or being able to ripen in a shorter growing season.

cash crops crops such as coffee that are grown specifically for direct sale or export.

commodity an agricultural commodity is a substance traded solely on its price rather than quality, such as wheat, sugar or maize.

conservation the active management of the Earth's natural resources and the environment to ensure their quality is maintained and that they are wisely used.

cultivate to grow crops.

economy the supply of money gained by a community or country from goods and services.

export any good or service that is sold outside the country in which it originates.

Fair Trade a movement in which organisations negotiate a fair price with the growers that will allow them to cover the costs and have a surplus for investment and living reasonably.

fertilisers chemicals or natural products added to soil that help plants and crops grow.

fossil fuels natural resources from the Earth that are non-renewable, such as coal and oil.

free trade trade that takes place without the presence of tariffs or subsidies, and is based on the price people are willing to pay.

GATT the General Agreement on Tariffs and Trade, established in 1948. It was succeeded in 1995 by the World Trade Organisation.

genetic modification the process of making some food products bigger, better, or more resistant to disease through combining the genes of different species to develop the strongest characteristics.

globalisation the rapid increase in cross-border economic, social and technological exchange.

global warming the phenomenon by which the Earth is growing gradually warmer as increasing amounts of greenhouse gases are released into the atmosphere by the burning of fossil fuels.

import any good or service that originates outside the country in which it is purchased.

intensive farming farming in which the maximum number of crops and livestock are raised on large areas of land.

less economically developed country (LEDC) one of the poorer countries of the world. LEDCs include all of Africa, Asia (except for Japan), Latin America and the Caribbean, and Melanesia, Micronesia and Polynesia.

mixed farming farming that produces a range of products, including plant and animal husbandry.

monoculture a farming system in which only one crop is grown, such as bananas or wheat.

more economically developed country (MEDC) one of the richer countries of the world. MEDCs include all of Europe, northern America, Australia, New Zealand and Japan.

multinational companies companies that operate in many countries and can move their products, personnel, and even factories to the location that is the most profitable.

quota a limit on the amount of produce that can be imported into a country. Often used to protect domestic producers from cheaper or competing imported goods.

shelf life how long a food product can last before it goes off.

staple a basic foodstuff such as wheat or maize.

subsidies grants of money made by the government to either a domestic seller or a buyer to help pay their costs of producing and selling certain goods and services.

surplus a quantity of a product that is larger than required.

sustainable development development that meets the needs of the present without compromising the ability of future generations to meet their own needs.

tariff a tax placed on goods transported from one country to another, or when imported. A tariff raises the price of imported goods, making them less competitive with locally produced goods.

World Trade Organisation (WTO) the organisation that administers trade agreements, provides a forum for trade negotiations, and monitors national trade policies for the 150 member countries. The overall aim of the WTO is to reach a single set of rules for trade.

yield the amount of crops that a farmer can produce.

Index

Africa 6, 7, 12, 26
agribusiness 30
Amazon 22
American National Farmers Union 15
animals 9, 15, 20, 21, 23, 26, 27, 34, 38, 40, 41
Asia 7, 9, 20, 21, 25
Asia-Pacific Economic Co-operation Forum 13

bananas 26, 27, 32
biodiversity 17, 30
biofuels 23
biotechnology 32, 33, 38, 39
Bové, José 37
Burger King 18

Café Direct 32
Cairns Group 13, 29
Canada 10, 13, 27
Caribbean 26
cash crops 19
China 41
climate conditions 8, 11, 16, 30, 36, 38
cocoa 10, 25, 26
coffee 10, 19, 24, 26, 32, 33
commodities 8, 10, 11, 24, 25, 26
conservation 14, 23
co-operatives 19

depots 9, 28

eggs 8, 21
environment 7, 9, 16, 17, 20, 29, 30, 38, 39
Equal Exchange 32
Ethiopia 11, 19
Europe 7, 8, 9, 12, 13, 22, 28, 29, 32, 33, 35
European Commission 33
European Union 13, 21, 29
exports 21, 26, 27

Fair Trade 31, 32, 33
Fairtrade Labelling Organisations International 32
Famine Early Warning System 11
farmers markets 29
fertilisers 9, 14, 19, 34, 38
fish 8, 35
FoodAid 23
food aid 11, 36
Food and Agriculture Organisation 36
food miles 9

food processing 27
fossil fuels 9
free trade 12–17, 19, 20, 21, 29, 30, 36, 41
fruit 8, 24

G20 13
General Agreement on Tariffs and Trade 16
genetic modification 16, 17, 18, 33, 38
global warming 9, 17, 28
globalisation 6, 7, 12, 19, 20, 27, 28, 30, 34, 35, 36, 37, 40, 41
governments 8, 11, 12, 14, 16, 17, 19, 20, 26, 29, 33
Greenpeace 22

healthcare 20, 26
hunger 36, 37

imports 8, 14, 20, 25, 27, 35
Indonesia 23, 35, 41
intensive farming 21, 29, 41
International Federation of Organic Agriculture Movements 17, 35
International Food Information Council 32

Latin America 7, 9, 25, 26
LEDCs 6, 7, 12, 17, 21, 26, 31, 32, 36
livestock 9, 34

maize 10, 24, 38
McDonald's 22, 37
meat 8, 24, 29
MEDCs 6, 7, 8, 14, 17, 19, 32, 36
Mexico 13, 32
mixed farming 17, 19
monocultures 17, 27
Monsanto 17
multinationals 7, 16, 22, 23, 25, 37

New Zealand 9, 29
North America 7, 9, 10, 13, 29, 35
North American Free Trade Agreement 13

organic farming 17, 31, 34, 35

palm oil 22, 23, 26, 27
Philippines 23
plantations 12, 22, 23, 26
populations 6, 14, 36, 37
pressure groups 20, 21, 30, 33
profits 12, 15, 20, 32

quotas 14

rationing 13
rice 10, 20, 29, 35, 40

Second World War 13, 14
seeds 8, 17, 38
shelf life 9, 35
soil 8, 16, 30, 34, 36, 40
Southeast Asia 22
soya 22, 24, 38
spices 12
staple foods 10
Starbucks 7
subsidies 11, 14, 15, 17, 20, 21, 29
sugar 10, 12, 24, 25, 26, 27
supermarkets 6, 9, 18, 23, 25, 28, 31, 32, 40
supply and demand 11, 25
surpluses 11, 15, 16, 21, 29, 36
sustainable development 23, 30, 31, 41
Switzerland 32

tariffs 11, 12, 14, 20, 21, 25
taxes 12, 25
tea 10, 26, 27
technology 6, 36, 39
Thailand 23
trade 6, 7, 12, 13, 14, 22, 24–25
    agreements 8, 13
    barriers 12, 14, 20, 21, 25, 30
    blocs 13
    rules 7, 16, 17
transportation 8, 9, 10, 28

Unilever 23
United Kingdom 32
United Nations 26
United Natural Foods 32
United States 13, 20, 21, 32
US Agency for International Development 11

vegetables 8, 9, 10, 24
vested-interest groups 15, 18

wheat 10, 13, 24, 29, 36, 38, 41
wildlife 17, 19, 20
World Trade Organisation 16, 17, 20, 21, 34, 41

yields 15, 35, 38, 41